Intermediate 2

INTERPRETATION PASSAGES

Model Papers

by

H.J. Davidson

ISBN 0 7169 6020 6

ROBERT GIBSON · Publisher

17 Fitzroy Place, Glasgow, G3 7SF.

www.gibson-books.co.uk

CONTENTS

INTRODUCTION

These tests are intended as practice for the Higher Still Examination in English and Communication. They are set at the level of the Intermediate 2 Interpretation / Close Reading Paper. You will have already taken a Close Reading paper for Standard Grade and will have some idea of the sort of questions that might be asked. The questions set for Intermediate 2 are more difficult and require more detailed analysis.

To help you and to give a clear indication of the purpose of the questions and the type of answers required a letter has been put beside the mark for each question.

U — Understanding: this means that you must show that you have understood **what** the writer is saying

A — Analysis: this means that you must pick out and explain the techniques that the writer has used to put across his ideas in an interesting or thought-provoking way. You must explain **how** he has said what he has to say.

E — Evaluation: this means you must decide for yourself **how well** the writer has expressed his views. You must refer to the passage and spport your opinion with evidence from the passage.

The number of marks given for each question indicates the length of answer expected.

Answer schemes are provided at the back of the book for the first two tests. You should attempt the tests before looking at the answers. They give an indication of what is required by the different type of questions. They also give an indication of the amount of detail required in your answers. You should try to mark your own answers so that you can see what you have missed out and work out for yourself the correct approach.

There are ten tests and they are all of a similar standard. The last one is possibly slightly more difficult than the earlier ones but by the time you have worked your way through the book you should be able to tackle it easily.

NATIONAL
QUALIFICATIONS

Time: 60 minutes

ENGLISH AND
COMMUNICATION
INTERMEDIATE 2
Interpretation

You should attempt all questions.

The total value of the Paper is 30 marks.

The passage that follows was written by Jeremy Hodges, a freelance writer.

Read the passage carefully and then answer **all** the questions, **using your own words as far as possible**.

The questions will ask you to show that:

- you understand the main ideas and important details in the passage — in other words, **what** the writer has said (**Understanding — U**).

- you can identify, using appropriate terms, the techniques the writer has used to get across these ideas — in other words, **how** he has said it (**Analysis — A**).

- you can, using appropriate evidence, comment on how effective the writer has been — in other words, **how well** he has said it (**Evaluation — E**).

A code letter (U, A, E) is used alongside each question to make clear its purpose to you. The number of marks attached to each question will give you some idea of the length of answer expected.

This article, by Jeremy Hodges, is about the Scotsman, Kirkpatrick Macmillan, who invented the first bicycle.

For a man whose invention was to revolutionise transport and put cheap travel in the grasp of ordinary people worldwide, Kirkpatrick Macmillan did not get off to a good start. When the Scottish blacksmith brought the world's first bicycle to Glasgow, he was arrested and flung in jail.

5　In 1842, when Macmillan rode into what was then Gorbals village, incredulous masses mobbed him as he pedalled his ungainly machine down the road. Mounting the pavement to avoid them, he inadvertently struck a little girl as she ran from a doorway.

She was no more than grazed, but it caused a furore — and within minutes Macmillan and his 'powered velocipede' were in police custody, charged with the early Victorian equivalent of
10　driving without due care and attention.

He had come to Glasgow in the hope of finding a rich entrepreneur who could capitalise on his invention. But instead of fame and fortune, he had brought notoriety and ridicule to his humble family in Dumfriesshire, not to mention shame and embarrassment on his brother, a respectable high school classics master, who had to come to bail him out.

15　Next day the *Glasgow Herald* reported how Macmillan was fined five shillings, and described his velocipede, adding dryly: 'To make it "progress" appeared to require more labour than will be compensated for by the increase of speed. The invention will not supersede the railways.'

What the *Herald* did not report was that after the hearing the magistrate requested a
20　demonstration of the machine in the courtyard outside — and was so impressed that he insisted on paying Macmillan's fine himself.

Nonplussed, Macmillan rode his machine home a few days later — winning a bet with a coach driver that he could beat the Royal Mail back to Sanquhar — and spent the rest of his life in happy obscurity.

25　He reaped no benefit and for many years was given no credit for inventing a machine that has since sold by the billion as a cheap, efficient and healthy means of getting from A to B.

The first pedal-driven bicycles were supposed to have been made in the 1860s by Michaux in Paris. The Ordinary or Penny Farthing came along about 1870, but in the official history of the bicycle there is little mention of Kirkpatrick Macmillan.

30　Yet the world's first bicycle emerged from the Courthill smithy owned by Macmillan's father in the parish of Keir, Dumfriesshire, towards the end of 1839 — a full 20 years ahead of the competition.

With its wooden frame and wheels, the rear one fitted with a crank and driven like a steam locomotive via iron rods connected to two swinging levers pushed to and fro by the feet, it
35 weighed half a hundredweight — but it worked.

Its inventor was a kindly, practical man, well-liked by the villagers who nevertheless regarded his streak of genius as a mark of insanity and promptly christened him 'Daft Pate'.

Born in 1812, the youngest son of James Macmillan and Mary Auld, he did not have the academic leanings of his elder brothers John and George, who both won places at Glasgow
40 University and became schoolmasters at Glasgow High School and Hutchesons' Grammar School respectively.

Young Pate was barely six when the hobby horse craze struck London in 1818. Patented by the German Karl van Drais, the Laufmaschine (running machine) or Draisienne was the forerunner of the bicycle. It had no pedal mechanism and was propelled forward by pushing with the feet
45 on the ground.

In England it was known as the hobby horse, and soon every smart young gentleman had to have one. News spread north, and, as an eight-year-old, Pate was fascinated to hear tales of the weird machines.

But it was not until he was 23, working as a blacksmith for the Duke of Buccleuch at nearby
50 Drumlanrig Castle, that he actually got to see a hobby horse. Immediately he and his friend John Findlater decided to make one for themselves, and in 1837 their bizarre contraption was the talk of the village.

The next stage in the development of the bicycle required a leap of imagination to the thought that you could balance on two wheels and propel yourself with some kind of mechanism.

55 It took a Scottish blacksmith to figure it out. Nobody knows how the idea came to Macmillan — perhaps he was inspired by early steam locomotives — but in 1839 every spare minute of his time was spent in the smithy, turning his ideas into practical reality.

The 'devilish machine' that emerged was greeted with cries of fear and horror by the villagers, who declared: 'The laddie's daft.' But they changed their tune when Macmillan, a strong man
60 standing 6ft 2in tall, managed to pedal his clumsy machine to Dumfries, a journey of 14 miles, within an hour.

Despite the unfortunate outcome of his trip to Glasgow, Macmillan's failure to turn his invention into a commercial success did not seem to bother him too much. He did not bother to patent the design and seems to have done very little with it.

65 But Gavin Dalzell, of Lesmahagow, and Thomas McCall, of Kilmarnock, had both seen Macmillan's contraption and shamelessly sold their own version for £7 each. In the 1840s, £7 was worth well over £1,000 in today's money and they made a tidy sum.

Eventually the Lion Bicycle Company in Coventry mass-produced the 'Dalzell Bicycle', which was essentially Macmillan's design and for which he received not a penny.

70   Yet Macmillan was happy to make copies for his friends for no more than the cost of the materials. After being invited to demonstrate his machine at a garden party at Drumlanrig Castle, he made one as a present for the Duke of Buccleuch — who ordered a second, and had to insist on paying for it.

Macmillan was never a rich man. He made no money from his invention, but set great store by
75   his friends, from wealthy landowners to the humblest child. When he died in 1878, there were hundreds at his funeral.

© Jeremy Hodges

QUESTIONS

Marks Code

1. Why might what is spoken of in paragraph 1 be described as ironical? 2 U

2. Look at lines 5–7. How does the word choice help us to realise how difficult the first bicycle was to control? 2 A

3. Look carefully at paragraph 4 (lines 11–14).

   (i) In your own words, explain what Macmillan had hoped to gain from his journey to Gorbals, Glasgow? 1 U

   (ii) In your own words, explain the effect it had on his family. 3 U

4. Explain the significance of the magistrate's actions after the court case (lines 19–21). 2 U

5. Look carefully at paragraph 11 (lines 33–35). How does the sentence structure help to emphasise the point the writer is trying to make about the bicycle? 2 A

6. Look at lines 42–48.

   Explain why you think that the 'hobby horse' was given that name? 2 A

7. Which word in paragraph 16 (lines 49–52) sums up the general opinion of the 'hobby horse' made by Macmillan and his friend? 1 A

8. How does the word choice and imagery of paragraph 19 (lines 58–61) make clear to us people's reaction to the machine? 4 A

9. Look at lines 65–67.

   How does the writer make clear his attitude towards Gavin Dalzell and Thomas McCall? 2 A

10. From your reading of the passage as a whole and in your own words explain any **TWO** benefits that were to be gained from the bicycle. 2 U

Marks Code

11. How well does the writer make clear his liking for the character of Kirkpatrick Macmillan in this article? **3**   **E**

12. How well in your opinion has the writer Jeremy Hodges demonstrated his skill in presenting the early history of the bicycle?

Justify your answer by referring to, for example, use of detail, word choice and imagery, sentence structure, etc. **4**   **E**

Total   **(30)**

NATIONAL
QUALIFICATIONS

Time: 60 minutes

ENGLISH AND
COMMUNICATION
INTERMEDIATE 2
Interpretation

You should attempt all questions.

The total value of the Paper is 30 marks.

The passage that follows was taken from an article in the *Scotland on Sunday* newspaper discussing the discovery by the writer of black bin bags in his car door.

Read the passage carefully and then answer **all** the questions, **using your own words as far as possible**.

The questions will ask you to show that:

- you understand the main ideas and important details in the passage — in other words, **what** the writer has said (**Understanding — U**).

- you can identify, using appropriate terms, the techniques the writer has used to get across these ideas — in other words, **how** he has said it (**Analysis — A**).

- you can, using appropriate evidence, comment on how effective the writer has been — in other words, **how well** he has said it (**Evaluation — E**).

A code letter (U, A, E) is used alongside each question to make clear its purpose to you. The number of marks attached to each question will give you some idea of the length of answer expected.

Opening the door to a weird use of bin bags

James May

My subject this week is one that has troubled me for some years — the bin bag and its untold contribution to the history and development of the world motor industry.

Few things in life are as indispensable as the humble bin bag, which is something of a paradox given that it is actually designed first and foremost to be put in a bin. I've just moved house.
5   The telly and the hi-fi are still inextricably subsumed under bubblewrap and piles of suitcases, but within minutes of entering my new dwelling, I'd opened the box containing the bin bags and embarked on an orgy of disposal.

A bin bag can also function as a temporary window while you wait for the real one to be replaced. Bin bags can be used as insulation for motorcycle couriers' feet in winter. If times are
10   hard, a mildly modified bin bag makes an effective and stylish raincoat. And while there is any real rubbish in the world, a bin bag will never be thrown away *per se*.

But there's something a bit weird going on with bin bags in the car business.

I was reminded of as much the other day by my friend, Sarah, who is one of those increasingly rare people who hasn't bothered to learn to drive. As a result, she's never been through that
15   character-building car-mending phase of early adulthood. A week ago, however, a window-winding mechanism on her bloke's Mazda came adrift, and she found herself in that time-honoured wifely tool-handing role. She takes up the story: 'When the trim panel came off I couldn't believe it. It was horrible inside. It was just bits of bent wire and plastic, and the paint is all rough and nasty. It's appalling. It looked like a *Blue Peter* car. And . . .' *elipsis*

20   And this is the bit that interests me.

'. . . there was a bin bag stuck over the inside of the door.'

I suddenly remembered a similar moment in my own late teens, when the door lock became detached on my first car, a Vauxhall Cavalier Mk 1, God rest its bones. I removed the interior panel, and there was a bin bag glued to the inside of the door with something like blutack. Once
25   you've pulled it off it never goes back on properly, and it always tears somewhere. In my innocence I cut a new bin bag to shape and reapplied it with Bostik, without really understanding why I was doing it.

Winding my motoring life's odometer forward to 1994, we arrive at the time when I owned an Alfa Romeo 164 and — you've probably guessed — the interior door handle broke. This time,
30   though, I was in a position to submit the car to an Alfa dealer for repair. It came back the next day and the door, and indeed the rest of the car, worked perfectly.

But a week or so later I was hoovering the inside of the Alfa and noticed a bin bag stuck to the back of the driver's seat with something like spent chewing gum. At first I was completely baffled, until I realised that it was the bin bag from inside the driver's door, which a mechanic had slapped there whilst at work, and then completely forgotten. The thing is, its absence made no difference whatsoever to the working of the door or the general refinement of the car's cabin.

And so, for perhaps the first time in history, I put a bin bag in the bin, inside the bin bag that was already there, fulfilling its rightful function.

So far, then, car-makers from Hiroshima to Luton to Arese are concealing bin bags inside car doors for no apparent reason. Is there, perhaps, a surfeit of unwanted bin bags in the new, paperless offices of the planet's car manufactuaries? Are these non-biodegradable items being disposed of by the back door, or even inside all the doors, to preserve these companies' ecologically sound images? Given the rate at which Mazdas, Vauxhalls and Alfas are produced, this system would account for a lot of bin bags.

But no, because the problem, I'm sorry to have to report, also extends to that last bastion of hand-built British charm, the Bentley Motor Cars trim shop.

Some weeks ago, I was charged with reviving, with the help of specialist trim restorers, the tired interior of Top Gear Magazine's aged Turbo R. I removed the four beautifully inlaid door cappings for re-lacquering. I then, with trembling hand, unscrewed the hidebound expanse of each interior trim panel for re-nourishment. And there, inside every door, was a bin bag. Not a bespoke Connolly Leather empty caviar jar disposal bag or anything like that, just a normal bin bag secured with something like congealed cheese sauce.

And what I want to know, what I have wanted to know ever since that seminal Vauxhall moment almost 20 years ago, is this.

Why?

© James May

QUESTIONS

Marks Code

1. Explain the <u>tone</u> of the opening sentence ('My subject this week . . .').   2   A

2. What is the '<u>paradox</u>' described in the second paragraph?   2   U

3. 'inextricably subsumed' (line 5)
    'orgy of disposal' (line 7)

    How does each of these phrases help to create the atmosphere of moving house?   4   A

4. What is the function of paragraph 4 (line 12)?   2   A

5. Look at the character of Sarah as depicted between lines 13–17. In what way is
    she typical of a modern woman and in what way not?   2   U

6. Look at the sentence structure in lines 19–21 ('And . . . door')

    How effective do you find the way the writer has written these sentences?   2   E

    long .... short ?

7. Explain what the expression 'God rest its bones' (line 23) tells us is the author's
    attitude to his first car?   2   A

8. Explain the writer's reference to his innocence in lines 25–26?   2   U

9. Look at lines 40–45

    What does the writer suggest is the real reason for the bin bags being used inside
    car doors?   2   U

10. Look at lines 48-53.

    (i)   How does the word choice help to create the writer's attitude to the Bentley
          car?   2   A

    (ii) How does the writer use word choice to make his point about the bin bag
          inside the Bentley's door?   2   A

11. How effective do you find the final one word paragraph as a conclusion to this article? 2 E

12. In this passage the writer is trying to discuss a not very serious issue in an entertaining way.

4 E

By commenting on at least **TWO** techniques explain how well you think he has achieved his purpose.

Total **(30)**

MODEL PAPER C

NATIONAL
QUALIFICATIONS

Time: 60 minutes

ENGLISH AND
COMMUNICATION
INTERMEDIATE 2
Interpretation

You should attempt all questions.

The total value of the Paper is 30 marks.

The passage that follows was taken from an article in *The Scotsman* which discusses the possible dangers of using mobile phones.

Read the passage carefully and then answer **all** the questions, **using your own words as far as possible**.

The questions will ask you to show that:

- you understand the main ideas and important details in the passage — in other words, **what** the writer has said (**Understanding — U**).

- you can identify, using appropriate terms, the techniques the writer has used to get across these ideas — in other words, **how** he has said it (**Analysis — A**).

- you can, using appropriate evidence, comment on how effective the writer has been — in other words, **how well** he has said it (**Evaluation — E**).

A code letter (U, A, E) is used alongside each question to make clear its purpose to you. The number of marks attached to each question will give you some idea of the length of answer expected.

If it's good to talk, why all the scares over health?

by

Camillo Fracassini

You're a parent and your 12-year-old daughter has told you exactly what she wants for her birthday next week.

It sounds like a good idea. All she is asking
5 for is something that will help you to keep tabs on her when she is out late or lost. But, according to some scientists whose work is being taken seriously by the government, the present she has in mind could make
10 your daughter suffer from memory loss. Some even claim that it could lead on to cancer and Alzheimer's disease

We are talking, in case you hadn't guessed, about mobile phones. In today's school
15 playgrounds, they are the ultimate status symbol.

Today, though there is as yet no definite evidence about the exact health risk that mobile phones pose, the government is
20 expected to issue urgent guidelines aimed at restricting the use of them by children.

This follows an alarming report by leading scientists which suggests that the devices pose an increased risk to young people.
25 Children are believed to be more susceptible because their skulls are thinner, allowing their brains to absorb more radiation.

The Stewart report, commissioned by the
30 government and led by Professor Sir William Stewart of Dundee University, is expected to recommend a minimum age for mobile phone use, a limit on the length and number of calls made by
35 children and calls for research into the potential damage to health caused by mobile phones. How such guidelines could be enforced is, of course, far more problematic.

40 Though the expected recommendations of

the Stewart report are precautionary, and are not based on conclusive evidence of an increased risk to children, most parents will move swiftly in an attempt to protect
45 their offspring from any danger.

Nevertheless, it may be almost impossible for them to halt the relentless march of technology. Already a quarter of mobile phone sales are to young people.

50 Three per cent of new subscribers are under 16 and it has been predicted that half of school pupils will be mobile phone users within the next three years.

This may be an underestimate. Most
55 children are already thoroughly immersed in internet technology and mobile phones will be the launch-pad to the future.

Mobile phones are already far more than devices merely designed for
60 communication.

The current generation of GSM mobile phones fitted with wireless application protocol (WAP) software allow users to surf the internet on the move, download
65 information from the web and trade e-mails.

But this is nothing compared with the potential of the third generation phones which will be at the heart of a
70 technological revolution. These devices promise to make PCs and the mobile phone that most of us are familiar with redundant. They will offer video, television, music and computer games on the move —
75 applications of particular appeal to children and teenagers.

Scientists are already warning that these phones will pose an even greater risk to health because they will emit more microwaves.

80 If these allegations are to be believed, the internet revolution might not be without casualties unless concerted action is taken to provide us with conclusive, independent research into the potential health risks 85 posed by mobiles.

Unfortunately, over the past few years we have been subjected to claim and counterclaim, fed a diet of hype, scare stories and conjecture.

90 Scientists have claimed that microwave radiation may heat and damage brain cells because mobile phones are held close to the head. Some experts have gone as far as to allege that making a ten-minute call on a 95 mobile is tantamount to putting your head in a microwave and have called for the devices to carry health warnings.

One scientist who believes there is cause for concern is Professor Henry Lai, of the 100 University of Washington, Seattle. Prof. Lai claimed his research had shown that exposure to radiation similar to that emitted by mobile phones had caused damage to the DNA strands in rats' brain 105 cells.

Responding to assurances from mobile phone manufacturers that the radiation emitted by their devices was safe, he replied: 'I cannot agree at all with what 110 they're telling the public. There is a concern and probably it's not safe.'

Other scientists have taken a more moderate line, suggesting that normal mobile phone use does not pose a danger 115 unless there is prolonged use such as 20 to 30 minute sessions, or total use of more than two hours a day. No sooner had the claims been made than other experts began to dismiss the claims as unsubstantiated 120 scaremongering.

The Federation of the Electronics Industry, which represents mobile phone manufacturers, has insisted that using a mobile phone poses no threat to human 125 health. It claims that £37·5 million of research carried out by the mobile phone industry world-wide has established no evidence of a link between using the devices and ill health.

130 Nevertheless, in an effort to reduce the potential risk, many owners bought hand-free kits believing that by keeping the devices away from their heads they would limit their exposure to microwaves.

135 Last month we were told the opposite might be true. According to research carried out by the Consumers' Association, the use of earpieces might actually amplify the energy and channel it directly in to the 140 users' heads. It claimed that the earpieces acted like aerials, directing up to three times as much radiation into the brain as a phone held up to your ear.

Commenting on the likely outcome of the 145 Stewart report, Alasdair Philips, of the consumer group Powerwatch, said: 'Our understanding is that the report will state that, for the majority of people, reasonable mobile phone use should not cause any 150 adverse health consequences, but that the jury is still out on possible links with a variety of effects including headaches, earaches, skin problems, concentration and short-term memory problems.'

155 In short, there is no conclusive evidence one way or the other.

Although the IACR's study may provide us with a definite answer, three years is a long time for mobile phone users to wait. It is 160 even longer for parents who are agonising over the potential damage that mobile phones may cause to their children. In the absence of decisive evidence, they might be best advised to adhere to the maxim 165 better safe than sorry.

© *The Scotsman*, 11 May 2000

QUESTIONS

Marks Code

1. Look at lines 1–28.

   (i) What are the benefits to children of mobile phones?   **1**   **U**

   (ii) What are the dangers?   **2**   **U**

   (iii) Why are children more at risk than adults?   **2**   **U**

2. Why do you think the writer waits until the third paragraph before telling us that he is writing about mobile phones.   **1**   **A**

3. Look at the two images:
   'relentless march of technology' (lines 47–48)
   'launch-pad to the future' (line 57).

   What do they suggest to you about the development of mobile phones?   **4**   **A**

4. Look at lines 70–79.

   Why does the writer think that 'the third generation' of phones will cause even greater problems for children?   **2**   **U**

5. Look at lines 90–120.

   Explain two contrasting views held by different groups of people about the dangers of mobile phones.   **2**   **U**

6. How does the imagery and word choice (lines 80–83) help to make clear the problem of finding out the truth of the dangers of mobile phones?   **4**   **A**

7. How effective do you find the image of 'putting your head in a microwave' (lines 95–96) in presenting the fears of those who see mobile phones as dangerous?   **2**   **A**

8. Look at lines 123–131.
   135–140

   Explain in your own words the problem discovered about 'hand-free kits' purchased by worried owners.   **2**   **U**

9. Explain the function of the second last paragraph (lines 155–156).   **1**   **A**

Marks Code

10. How effective do you find the headline as an introduction to this article?

    Comment on sentence structure and word choice.   **3**   **E**

11. Would the way this article has been presented put you off using a mobile phone?   **4**   **E**

                                                            Total   **(30)**

NATIONAL
QUALIFICATIONS

Time: 60 minutes

ENGLISH AND
COMMUNICATION
INTERMEDIATE 2
Interpretation

You should attempt all questions.

The total value of the Paper is 30 marks.

The passage that follows was taken from an article in *The Times* newspaper discussing the practice being developed by large companies of sending employees on staff bonding weekends.

Read the passage carefully and then answer **all** the questions, **using your own words as far as possible**.

The questions will ask you to show that:

- you understand the main ideas and important details in the passage — in other words, **what** the writer has said (**Understanding — U**).

- you can identify, using appropriate terms, the techniques the writer has used to get across these ideas — in other words, **how** he has said it (**Analysis — A**).

- you can, using appropriate evidence, comment on how effective the writer has been — in other words, **how well** he has said it (**Evaluation — E**).

A code letter (U, A, E) is used alongside each question to make clear its purpose to you. The number of marks attached to each question will give you some idea of the length of answer expected.

THE TIMES   Friday, May 12, 2000

The **height** of nonsense

Mountain climbing to build corporate team spirit will never work,
says Julian Champkin

Some companies look after their staff. They give them rewards for achievement: bonuses, Caribbean holidays, or gold watches. Other companies make their staff undergo ritual starvation, exhaustion and humiliation to make them work hard. They call this corporate bonding.

5   It is an odd concept, this. Take a nice, ordinary working group of suburban men and women. Send them on a hard, tough, terrifying adventure — braving bitter-cold seas and winds on the northern tip of Scotland, for example; or strand them in the middle of Dartmoor with nothing but a rabbit that they have to catch, kill and gut between them before they can eat. Or make them walk barefooted across red-hot coals. That one really has happened on a work-loyalty

10   weekend.

The idea is that shared painful experiences build group bonds and team spirit with your work-mates. If this ghastly medieval horror were applied to criminals, the Court of Human Rights would be up in arms.

Anne Shackley did take her company to court after she was forced to dress up in a sumo suit

15   to wrestle a colleague. Sumo wrestling with colleagues would, according to the pea-brain who sent the sales force on this horror exercise, encourage 'team-building' and was 'part of the new corporate culture'.

Instead Miss Shackley, a slightly built woman, over-balanced, hit her head and developed epilepsy. Her company has had to pay her £275,000 compensation; and serve them right.

20   The concept of owing personal loyalty to a vast, impersonal company is an odd one. Owing loyalty to a company that inflicts such treatments is verging on the downright perverted.

Of course, the concept of bonding through torture is insane. Adventures, hard physical adventures, are for people who like such things. The one thing they do not encourage is team spirit. Shared hardships do not make for shared loyalties. What they actually make for is

25   bitterness, hatred and rancour.

Sending people to climb mountains is a popular corporate bonding exercise — after all, when you are all on the same rope, you literally need each other to survive. But this ignores the fact that good mountaineers are, on the whole, the most selfish band of individualists who have ever inhabited the universe. They quite literally step over the dead bodies of their comrades to get

30   to the top.

I once accompanied a group to Everest. One of our party was weaker than the others; I innocently suggested that more oxygen might be bought for him. That way, more people might get to the top. I could not have made a greater social *faux pas*. A rage-filled meeting was summoned — and I was told firmly to stay outside the tent while it happened. 'If he gets more

35   oxygen than me, I'm walking out,' was just one furious reaction.

So, bonding on mountains? Pull the other. Certainly, now and then, mountaineers make great sacrifices to save each other's lives. But that doesn't make for mutual liking. A climbing expedition which returns with all its members still on speaking terms is an exception rather than a rule.

40   Mountaineering books about great mountaineering expeditions do not generally describe climbing mountains. They describe instead how selfish, unreasonable, vile and appalling the other members of the expedition were. They go on at length about who wanted to go it alone; how the base camp deteriorated into bickering and rows; how the squabbles as to who is to go in the advance party and who just carries the luggage, lead to walk-outs and rage. As soon as

45   mountaineers hit the airport on the way home they split up as quickly as possible and do not speak to each other until they need to climb the next mountain.

Adventure sailors sail single-handed round the world. The reason is obvious. If there were two on a boat, one would murder the other before the Beachy Head lighthouse was out of view.

I have been on that sort of boat, too. We were sailing, as it happens, to the Antarctic — ten of

50   us on a too-small yacht for six weeks. There were storms, we hit icebergs, we were way out of reach of any help and our liferaft went overboard one night.

We did at least have enough sense to realise that a flaming row on board would be disastrous — but we most desperately needed one.

As a pathetic substitute, we subsumed our rages in competitive cookery. If one person one night

55   produced a four-course meal, the next night someone else had to do an even better five-course one.

It was particularly pointless in that when sea-sick and exhausted in a force 10 gale, the last thing one wants is six courses with starters, aperitifs and a hand-written menu in French.

It became positively counter-productive in that we used so much bottled gas that it ran out and

60   for the last four days we had not so much as a cup of hot tea. And despite those desperate elastoplast bond-building techniques, one relationship which had seemed destined to result in marriage, ended the moment we stepped back on the quayside.

When conditions get tough, hatreds and loathings magnify. Adversity leads to strife. The smallest detail — who ate the last Smartie in the tube — leads to real feelings of violence, if

65   not actual blows. Yet big companies force reluctant employees to undergo such experiences in the fond hope that they will return better, happier and more loyal to the company.

They send whole finance departments to train with the Royal Marines. Although, one simple point seems to have escaped these big companies. If the financiers had wanted to be Marines, they would have joined the Army, not a company that makes jelly.

70   Worse even than corporate-imposed pain is corporate humiliation. Dress the sales department as clowns. Hold compulsory karaoke nights. A public limited company has, as a lawyer once said, neither a body to kick nor a soul to be damned. It follows that loyalty of body and soul is not something that it can, or should, demand.

People join companies for one simple reason: to earn enough to pay their mortgages and keep
75   their children fed and clothed. In return, they put up with moronic bosses. They turn up most days at nine or nine-thirty, work reasonably conscientiously, even at deadly boring jobs, and take a not excessive number of days' sick leave. That, surely, is loyalty enough and pretty good value for the money.

You want corporate bonding with it? First I'd like to see employers, dressed in rubber sumo
80   suits, facing pain and cold on a desolate mountainside.

© Julian Champkin / Times Newspapers Limited, 12th May 2000.

QUESTIONS

Marks Code

1. Look carefully at paragraph 1 (lines 1–4).

   (i) What is Julian Champkin's attitude to firms who make their staff go on adventure expeditions for the sake of corporate bonding?

   1 **U**

   (ii) Explain how the writer uses contrast and tone to make his opinion clear in the opening paragraph.

   4 **A**

2. How does the word choice in paragraph two (lines 5–10) make clear her attitude to adventure weekends?

   4 **A**

3. What problem for the companies themselves is highlighted by the story of Anne Shackley in lines 14–19?

   2 **U**

4. Look at lines 22–25.

   What underlying problem does he claim is the case when people share difficult and painful experiences?

   2 **U**

5. How does the sentence structure of line 36, 'So, bonding . . . the other', reinforce the tone of his words?

   3 **A**

6. Look at lines 40–46.

   How does the sentence structure combine with the word choice to create a picture of the character and behaviour of mountain climbers?

   4 **A**

7. How effective do you find the phrase 'elastoplast bond-building techniques' (line 61) to describe the aim of group adventures?

   2 **E**

8. Look at lines 68–69.

   Why do you think the writer placed his financiers in a company that makes jelly?

   2 **U**

9. What distinction is the writer making between 'pain' and 'humiliation' in line 70?

   2 **A**

10. How well has the writer used any of the following to put across his point of view?
- Imagery,
- tone,
- anecdote,
- sentence structure.   **4**   **E**

                                                                        Total   **(30)**

NATIONAL
QUALIFICATIONS

Time: 60 minutes

ENGLISH AND
COMMUNICATION
INTERMEDIATE 2
Interpretation

You should attempt all questions.

The total value of the Paper is 30 marks.

The passage that follows was taken from an article in *The Scotsman* newspaper and describes the problems caused by bears to campers in some areas of America.

Read the passage carefully and then answer **all** the questions, **using your own words as far as possible**.

The questions will ask you to show that:

- you understand the main ideas and important details in the passage — in other words, **what** the writer has said (**Understanding — U**).

- you can identify, using appropriate terms, the techniques the writer has used to get across these ideas — in other words, **how** he has said it (**Analysis — A**).

- you can, using appropriate evidence, comment on how effective the writer has been — in other words, **how well** he has said it (**Evaluation — E**).

A code letter (U, A, E) is used alongside each question to make clear its purpose to you. The number of marks attached to each question will give you some idea of the length of answer expected.

Don't feed the bears

A hungry visitor can turn a lazy camping trip into a fairly grizzly experience,
writes Tim Cornwell.

My brother, who lives in Ojai, a pretty country town safely outside the LA sprawl, swears that there are bears there who feast on avocados. They can be heard at night, he says, with loud slurping noises issuing from the avocado orchards as they devour the fruit.

5   My brother has six children and a screenwriter's imagination. But bears are indeed a hazard of life in parts of California and in particular when camping out. One close encounter, according to those who know, in which a bear wrecks your car or trashes your tent, can permanently alter your attitude to Yogi or Smokey.

Camping is a great way to see California. As a family, we only began camping recently and we do not have bear stories, yet. But plenty of our friends do.

10   'The first time you come nose-to-nose with a bear, it can make your skin quiver,' advises the California Camping guide.

In grizzly country further north, in Montana or over the border in Canada, wilderness walkers wear bear bells, like cow bells, on their packs. It ruins the peace and quiet, but it means the bears (particularly a mother and her cubs) don't get surprised. Others go equipped with bear 15   sprays, like the pepper sprays used to fend off unwanted people, though their effectiveness is hotly debated.

Tamer California has no grizzlies, but it does have the 'mild-mannered' common black bear by the score. They run from 250 to 400 lbs with large claws and teeth, and a good turn of speed. Confusingly, they are sometimes brown.

20   And they have become, as the guide book notes, 'specialists in the food-raiding business'.

Last year, in Yosemite National Park, black bears set a record when they clawed and crashed their way into more than 1,000 visitors' cars, smashing windows or peeling back the doors of vans and estates like tins of sardines to get at backpacks and cooler boxes. By inserting claws just above a rear door, it is reported, they can rip down the entire door frame.

25   The Yosemite bears showed a predilection for breaking into Hondas and Toyotas; one learned to hit vehicles while the owners were registering for the night. For the more solitary camper, off the beaten track, the risk is a hungry bear who turns a pleasant evening round the campfire into a hair-raising night in the tent.

Lisa Warner and her husband Nick, a British physicist in Los Angeles, whose children went to 30   pre-school with ours, had just such an experience. On the last night of a five-day camping trek a few years back, they had just finished up their freeze-dried turkey pasta 'when we heard this grunt, grunt, grunt,' Lisa said.

The bear they had encountered earlier that afternoon, stripping termites out of a log, had come in search of easier pickings — not them, but their food. An uneasy night followed, with the bear
35 prowling round their camp, frequently tripping over tent ropes and crashing into trees.

The protocol for dealing with a bear in the wild is to put all food, and anything that smells of it, in a bear-safe container a good distance from your tent. California camp sites in bear country often come with steel bear boxes, locked and bolted to the ground, to house food.

If a bear turns up, the trick is to let them know you are there, but in a non-threatening fashion.
40 In a tent, this apparently consists of turning on a torch and keeping up a low conversation, if you have the nerve.

A couple of years ago, Angela Wallace, her sister and mother decided — as a kind of spur of the moment thing — to go camping with four small children and one older child. They arrived late, in the Sequoia National Forest, and after they had set up, a bear came 'rumbling
45 by' she said.

The bear circled the camp, actually brushing past a five-year-old in another party roasting a marshmallow over a fire.

'Basically everybody freaked out,' remembered Wallace. 'We realised we couldn't even sleep in the car; they tear off the car doors.'

50 It was nearly a two hour drive to the nearest motel.

Black bears do not eat people: they simply want their food and are apt to act pretty cross if someone gets in their way. They are omnivores, and camping supplies is a fast-food alternative to old-fashioned foraging by digging for grubs or finding berries.

Bears that have developed a particular habit for raiding camps or cars, or which are spotted
55 teaching their cubs to do so, are typically put to sleep with a dart gun and released somewhere distant.

If they become repeat offenders, they may get a fatal dose. Bears involved in the very rare maulings are usually tracked down and killed.

'If they are stealing your food and you try to stop them, they are going to smack you or claw
60 you or bite you, who knows what,' said Jim Whitfield, an assistant recreational officer at Sequoia, a 1,700 square mile piece of the Sierra Nevada mountain range.

'Black bears are pretty bright, very determined, they will do almost anything. They will just as soon get food the easiest possible way they can.' In the wild, if bear boxes are not available, the recommended practice is to hang all food items — including toothpaste and shampoo,
65 which are known to smell particularly tempting — from the bough of a distant tree.

In some cases, though, bears are said to have launched themselves off branches in an attempt to reach the dangling pack. Whitfield came across a black bear and her cubs in the Sequoia National Forest this weekend, on a hunting trip.

'She sent the cubs up the trail and came to see what I was all about,' he said. The bear charged
70 him, and 'I hollered and she stopped and we sort of had a stand-off for a few minutes,'
Whitfield continued.

'Then we both agreed to go opposite directions.'

QUESTIONS

Marks Code

1. Look at lines 1–5.

    (i)   How has the writer's brother tried to make his story of bears seem realistic?   **2**   **A**

    (ii) Quote the phrase which suggests that the writer does not quite believe him.   **1**   **A**

2. What does the comma and the word 'yet' (line 9) suggest about the family's lack of bear stories?   **1**   **A**

3. Explain what the tone is of 'specialists in the food-raiding business' (line 20).   **2**   **A**

4. Look at lines 21–28.

    What evidence is there that bears are
    (i)   strong?
    (ii) intelligent?   **4**   **U**

5. Look at lines 36–41.

    What are the **TWO** main techniques for dealing with bears when camping?   **2**   **U**

6. Look at lines 51–53.

    Explain **ONE** technique used by the writer to add humour to his description of the bears' eating habits?   **2**   **A**

7. Look at lines 57–58.

    Under what conditions are bears actually killed?   **2**   **U**

8. Look at lines 62–65.

    How does the writer support the comment made by Jim Whitfield that 'Black bears are . . . very determined' in line 62?   **2**   **U**

9. How does the sentence structure help the story told by Whitfield in lines 69–72?   **2**   **A**

10. How effective do you find the headline and second headline in catching the reader's attention?

    2   **E**

11. Look at the two stories told about Lisa Warner (lines 29–35) and Angela Wallace (lines 42–50).

How well are the stories told, and which, in your opinion, is made to seem the more frightening?

  (i)   Lisa Warner (lines 29–35).

    4   **E**

  (ii) Angela Wallace (lines 42–50).

    4   **E**

                                    Total   **(30)**

NATIONAL
QUALIFICATIONS

Time: 60 minutes

ENGLISH AND
COMMUNICATION
INTERMEDIATE 2
Interpretation

You should attempt all questions.

The total value of the Paper is 30 marks.

The passage that follows was taken from an article in *The Scotsman* newspaper in which Ian Wood discusses the problems associated with athletes trying to relax and enjoy sport.

Read the passage carefully and then answer **all** the questions, **using your own words as far as possible**.

The questions will ask you to show that:

- you understand the main ideas and important details in the passage — in other words, **what** the writer has said (**Understanding — U**).

- you can identify, using appropriate terms, the techniques the writer has used to get across these ideas — in other words, **how** he has said it (**Analysis — A**).

- you can, using appropriate evidence, comment on how effective the writer has been — in other words, **how well** he has said it (**Evaluation — E**).

A code letter (U, A, E) is used alongside each question to make clear its purpose to you. The number of marks attached to each question will give you some idea of the length of answer expected.

Relaxation can really get on an athlete's nerves at times

Ian Wood: *A slice of life*

There's nothing like relaxation for getting sportspeople uptight. Relaxation is at the very heart of sport, which is unfortunate, for relaxing is the last thing a sportsperson straining to achieve maximum performance seems able to do.

5 Sport is awash with tight-lipped coaches telling tight-lipped charges to relax while lips get tighter by the minute.

This on-going conflict makes for some contradictory situations. At a football match in which the play was proving less than riveting, my attention wandered to the benches, where capered the managerial teams. It's a curious feature of the game these days that while players work themselves into a lather, the boys in the dug-outs drink gallons of water. Anyway, when they

10 weren't drinking water, the coaching staff were screaming at the players.

Of course, there was no telling what they were trying to tell them, but you got the impression they weren't imparting words of comfort and guidance.

At times it looked hostile and this was rather confirmed when the occupants of one dug-out began to direct their advice at a young-looking defender.

15 Now that he was getting their undivided attention, the player appeared to have retreated into a sullen and resentful state in which fear and confusion fought for supremacy.

As everyone seemed to be pointing in different directions, this was hardly surprising and the unlucky lad, having run out of ideas for ways of stemming the tirade, finally ran off, kicked a member of the opposition and was booked.

20 I suppose it was either that or digging a hole and jumping in.

Quite apart from the negative mental effects of this sort of treatment, can football really be played with an eye on the bench and the ears full of abuse?

After a week of presumably intensive training, what can be left for coaches to scream that hasn't been screamed already? Apart from all that, surely a pro footballer can figure out some

25 things for himself.

The mystery of this odd behaviour deepens when a boss comes away with the memorable phrase: 'I just told them to go out and enjoy themselves.'

Perhaps this was the message being conveyed to the defender. The bench might have been screaming something along the lines of: 'Jimmy, Jimmy — start enjoying yersel, ye wee

30 scunner,' but it certainly didn't look like it.

On much the same wave-length are pleas made by managements to supporters to get behind the team.

A staunch supporter, they say, is like having an extra man on the park. The pleas take on a hollow ring when, even as the crowd are responding, the members of the dug-out are doing
35 everything except throw bricks.

Relaxation doesn't have much of a chance in such a context. Golf is different, but much the same. Even golfers of average handicaps can settle to a rhythm during practice sessions and hit sequences of passable shots. This is because they are relaxed, there being no reason for them to be otherwise.

40 If there's a glitch or two it doesn't matter, they just carry on. The trouble is that the minute they slip the scorecards into their pockets, it is as if an alarm system has somehow been activated.

Muscles contract, eyes glaze over, palms sweat and the brain dies. They are as relaxed as a spiralling member of a free-fall team who has just noticed he's forgotten his parachute.

In many ways, it is harder to relax at golf than it is in football and the results of failure more
45 damaging, for each shot involves starting from cold.

There is no triggering action to respond to, no instinctive reaction to fall back on.

Most instinctive reactions in golf are bad, including as they do, lifting of the head, snatching of the wrists, stiffening of the legs, shutting of the eyes and whitening of the knuckles.

Not for nothing do the touring professionals flock to consult psychiatrists.

50 Should the handicap golfer ever begin to follow suit, it will be only a matter of time before their psychiatrists are flocking to consult other psychiatrists. It could all get pretty fraught.

I've often felt that a measure of relaxation might be induced by concentration on something other than the swing.

Course management, for instance.

55 The effort of planning some sort of strategy could take the strain off the business of actually hitting the shot.

With, say, the ideal line established as the priority and held firmly in mind, the swing might take care of itself. Recently, an acquaintance of mine seemed to be on the right track when, on the tee of a dangerous long par-4, he discarded a state-of-the-art driver he'd been trying out and
60 announced that in the interests of safety and accuracy he was reverting to his own driver.

This, I thought, sounded promising.

He hit a low, wounded shot out the heel into a small copse a few yards distant and the ball, after whining off various limbs and branches, came to rest in a hopeless lie in the roots of a tree.

Wearily, I watched another cherished theory bite the dust.

QUESTIONS

Marks Code

1. Explain the contradiction being described in the first paragraph.

   2   U

2. How does the word choice help to make the writer's point in paragraph 2 (lines 4–5)?

   3   A

3. What does the word 'capered' (line 7) suggest about the managerial teams the writer was watching?

   1   A

4. What does the story of the young defender in lines 13–19 contribute to the writer's argument?

   3   U

5. How does the style of the imagined words of the coach 'Jimmy, Jimmy . . . wee scunner' (lines 29–30) tell us what sort of person the writer imagines a coach to be?

   2   A

6. What is the difference between practising and playing golf?

   2   U

7. Look at lines 44–46.

   In your own words explain what the two aspects of golf are which make it even harder to relax than in football?

   2   U

8. How does the sentence structure help to make the writer's point clear in lines 49–51?

   2   A

9. Look at the paragraph in line 54.

   Comment on the structure and purpose of this paragraph.

   2   A

10. How does the style of lines 62–64 help to emphasise the bad shot hit by his acquaintance?

    4   A

11. How effective do you find the image of the free-fall parachutist in lines 42–43?

    3   E

12. The title tells us that relaxation 'can get on an athlete's nerves at times' which suggests he does not think relaxing is possible for athletes.

To what extent would you say the way he has written this article has helped to prove his point.

You should look at:
> word choice;
> sentence structure;
> imagery;
> sound effects;
> anecdotes;
> etc.   **4   E**

                                                               Total   (30)

MODEL PAPER G

NATIONAL QUALIFICATIONS	Time: 60 minutes	ENGLISH AND COMMUNICATION INTERMEDIATE 2 Interpretation

You should attempt all questions.

The total value of the Paper is 30 marks.

The passage that follows was taken from an article in *The Scotsman* about the large number of people over the age of fifty in this country at the moment.

Read the passage carefully and then answer **all** the questions, **using your own words as far as possible**.

The questions will ask you to show that:

- you understand the main ideas and important details in the passage — in other words, **what** the writer has said (**Understanding — U**).

- you can identify, using appropriate terms, the techniques the writer has used to get across these ideas — in other words, **how** he has said it (**Analysis — A**).

- you can, using appropriate evidence, comment on how effective the writer has been — in other words, **how well** he has said it (**Evaluation — E**).

A code letter (U, A, E) is used alongside each question to make clear its purpose to you. The number of marks attached to each question will give you some idea of the length of answer expected.

THE SCOTSMAN   8 May, 2000

Has the Age of Ageism had its day?

We can't afford to ditch so many of our knowledgeable citizens when they hit 50.

Gavin Esler

The Cult of Youth which has infected Britain since the Fifties is on the wane. It is not dead, but it may be mortally wounded. From the Fifties and youth cults such as Teddy Boys and bobbysoxers to the Sixties and Mods and Rockers, to Punks and Goths and New Romantics and all the rest, for 50 years the British media have been obsessed with the idea that vigour,
5   creativity, and spending power in our society are the prerogatives of the young.

By 'young' they mean those who are in their teens to their late twenties. The rest of the British population have been dismissed as wrinklies, set in their ways, happy never to try new experiences, fuddy-duddies in cardigans best left in front of the telly, oldsters to be reviled and pushed aside, retired from their jobs and left to mow lawns, clip hedges and complain about
10   their increasingly embarrassing personal maladies and intimate plumbing problems. The advertising industry remains one of the last strongholds of the cult of youth. It still tries to sell supposedly sexy products such as booze, cigarettes, fashions and cosmetics to the young, while the old are targeted for nothing more glamorous than head-ache cures, painkillers and Preparation H.

15   The Who used to sing the ultimate Youth Cult anthem, *Talkin' 'Bout My Generation*, with Roger Daltry wailing, 'I hope I die before I get old'. But now? Roger Daltry and Pete Townsend remain favourites of dinosaur rock, which still rules the planet. When asked to vote for our favourite rock singers in a survey last year, a granny came number one — Tina Turner, now 60. The youngest female vocalist in the survey was Madonna, forty-something. Other rock
20   wrinklies such as Eric Clapton, Led Zeppelin, Santana and the Stones all make the Most Favourite Artist lists, while the best worshippers at the Cult of Youth can come up with to dismay their elders are pasteurised, homogenised and genetically modified organisms known as Steps and any boy band you can think of.

The Henley Centre has produced statistics which show an increase in middle-aged thrill-
25   seeking in a nation of Richard Branson danger-lovers who have not grown up and should know better. In the five years from 1991, there was a 41 per cent increase in motorcycle accidents involving 30- to 40-year-olds, while accidents among the 17-19 age group fell by 57 per cent. Meanwhile, the Royal Geographical Society complains about a lack of spirit of adventure among British youngsters who are becoming risk-averse couch potatoes emblematic of a play-
30   safe youth culture.

Of course Britain remains an ageist society, as anyone over 50 trying to get a job will tell you. But faced with the most obvious demographic shock — that there are now 15 million

consumers in Britain over 50, that 80 per cent of this country's wealth is in the hands of those
over 45, and that the proportion of young people all across western Europe is set to fall
35 precipitately, even the dimmest of our large corporations and bureaucracies is beginning to
wake up to the value of age, experience and the Grey Pound.

The government has also spotted the problems ahead. We live in what Downing Street
recognises as a knowledge-based economy. So why does it make sense to push aside so many
of our most knowledgeable citizens when they hit 50, to make way for younger, cheaper but
40 inevitably less experienced replacements? It doesn't. And the demographic changes mean that
in 30 years' time too few young British workers could be paying to keep in retirement too many
old British wrinklies.

All this amounts to a waste of national expertise, which may lead to the removal of tax
advantages for those retiring at 50, an increase in the age of retirement, and a government
45 campaign to bludgeon the more stupid businesses into hiring or retaining older workers. In the
past year one chain of travel agents announced it intends to train older workers because most
of us would prefer to buy our summer holidays from people who have travelled around, rather
than some pimply youth who has been to Ibiza but who thought Gascony played for Rangers
before ending up at Middlesborough. B&Q, Sainsbury's, Domino's Pizza and Scottish
50 Equitable are among other companies who have targeted older workers as potential employees.

Besides if we adopt American trends, as we usually do, we are also witnessing an extraordinary
generational shift in this year's presidential election, the first in which both candidates are Baby
Boomers* with their formative years in the Sixties. As a fortysomething American woman
diplomat once put it to me when watching the first Baby Boomer president after Bill Clinton's
55 inauguration: 'The scary thing now is, it's my generation that's in charge.'

And of course this is the generation that never quite grew up and which still stumbles forward
with the confidence of a sleep-walker in its attempts to change the world. This same generation,
as it ages, will undoubtedly change the world once again to ensure a better deal for older people
on both sides of the Atlantic. Besides, Old just is not Old any more. If these trends continue,
60 then Old is the new Young.

Gavin Esler is a presenter on BBC News 24

*   *"Baby Boomers" are those people born after the 2nd World War, roughly between 1945
and 1960, when there was a huge number of babies born who all survived and grew up
in the sixties.*

© Gavin Esler

QUESTIONS

1. How does the imagery in lines 1–2 help us to understand the writer's thoughts on the 'Cult of Youth'?

2   A

2. Write down two quite different adjectives to sum up the general impression of 'wrinklies' suggested by the long description of them in lines 7–10.

2   A

3. What does the word 'supposedly' add to the meaning of the sentence beginning 'It still tries to sell . . .' (line 11)?

1   U

4. Look at paragraph 3 (lines 15–23).

   (i)   What is suggested by the term 'dinosaur rock' when used of Roger Daltrey and Pete Townsend?

2   A

   (ii)   Choose one of the expressions used about younger bands and explain what it suggests about the writer's attitude to them.

2   A

5. Look at lines 24–30.

   (i)   What does the evidence produced by the Henley Centre suggest about the old and the young?

2   U

   (ii)   What has the Royal Geographic Society to add to this argument?

2   U

6. Look at lines 31–36.

   (i)   What has been the vast change in the age statistics of Britain over the last few years?

2   U

   (ii)   What do you think is meant by the 'Grey Pound'?

1   U

   (iii)   Why should this be of interest to large corporations?

1   U

7. What does the word 'bludgeon' (line 45) suggest about the attitudes of some businesses?

2   A

8. What did a woman of forty find so strange about President Clinton's election as president?

2   U

Marks Code

9. Explain what the writer means by his last sentence.   2   U

10. 'The generation that still stumbles forward with the confidence of a sleep-walker in its attempts to change the world' (lines 56–57).

    What does the word choice in this sentence tell us about the writer's opinion of the generation that grew up in the sixties?   3   A

11. What characteristics of a newspaper article has the writer used to catch people's interest in what he has to say?   4   E

Total   **(30)**

NATIONAL
QUALIFICATIONS

Time: 60 minutes

ENGLISH AND
COMMUNICATION
INTERMEDIATE 2
Interpretation

You should attempt all questions.

The total value of the Paper is 30 marks.

The passage that follows was taken from an article in the *New Scientist* describing one of the secret gadgets provided for British airmen who might be shot down over enemy territory during World War 2.

Read the passage carefully and then answer **all** the questions, **using your own words as far as possible**.

The questions will ask you to show that:

- you understand the main ideas and important details in the passage — in other words, **what** the writer has said (**Understanding — U**).

- you can identify, using appropriate terms, the techniques the writer has used to get across these ideas — in other words, **how** she has said it (**Analysis — A**).

- you can, using appropriate evidence, comment on how effective the writer has been — in other words, **how well** she has said it (**Evaluation — E**).

A code letter (U, A, E) is used alongside each question to make clear its purpose to you. The number of marks attached to each question will give you some idea of the length of answer expected.

They look like ordinary pencils. And they write like ordinary pencils. It's the green paint that's the giveaway. These pencils, on display at the Cumberland Pencil Museum in Keswick, were made during the Second World War, when paint was in short supply and pencils left the factory with a natural wood finish. The paint marks them out as a special

5 line. Snap one open and all is revealed. Hidden inside is a map and a tiny compass.

The pencils, issued to British airmen flying over enemy territory, were one of the secret gadgets thought up by Charles Fraser-Smith, the shadowy civil servant who became the model for Ian Fleming's 'Q' in the James Bond stories. Like most of Fraser-Smith's ingenious devices, the pencils were made by a well-known manufacturer — the

10 Cumberland Pencil Company in this case. By using established firms, the man from the ministry was able to tap the ingenuity of a whole band of engineers and designers, and he ended up with a product bearing a well-known name that wouldn't arouse suspicions if it fell into the wrong hands.

Secret service

by Stephanie Pain

15 At 5·30 pm, Fred Tee picked up the folder with his papers in, put on his trilby and headed for home. Like most of the 100-strong workforce at the Cumberland Pencil Company, he was a local man and lived just a few minutes' walk from the factory in Keswick. As soon as it grew dark, Tee, the factory's youthful technical manager, set off back to the works and quietly let himself into his laboratory through the back door. This was the fifth night in a row that he and

20 his fellow managers had met after work to do a spot of moonlighting.

This was 1942, and Britain was at war. Tee and his colleagues had been asked to produce a special type of pencil: it must have a secret compartment just large enough to hold a tightly rolled map and a tiny compass. In the interests of security, only the managers were in on the secret, sworn to silence by the Official Secrets Act.

25 Tee and the Cumberland Pencil Company had been commissioned by a mysterious man from London who claimed to be a civil servant from the Ministry of Supply's Clothing and Textile Department. He was Charles Fraser-Smith. a fixer whose real job was to supply equipment and gadgets for MI6, MI9 and the Special Operations Executive — everything from miniature cameras to surgical saws, edible notepaper and forged foreign currency. He was always on the

30 lookout for novel ways to hide equipment that would help downed airmen avoid capture, prisoners of war escape, and secret agents get their information safely back to Britain. He was the original 'Q' immortalised in the James Bond movies.

Fraser-Smith was bombarded with requests for devices with secret compartments, and conjured up shaving brushes, pipes and pens, golf balls and even shoe laces that concealed escape

35 equipment. His strategy was to approach a well-known firm that made a suitable object and ask if they could make a version with some unusual features. Across Britain, designers and engineers took up the challenge.

So when Fraser-Smith needed a pencil with a secret compartment he visited the oldest manufacturer in the country, the Cumberland Pencil Company. Was it possible, he asked, to
40　make a pencil that would hold a tightly rolled map, about 12 centimetres long, plus a compass — without anyone noticing? A pencil was a standard piece of navigation equipment, making it an ideal place to hide escape gear.

As technical manager, Tee worked out how to make the pencils without the rest of the tight-knit community finding out about them. There were six separate operations in producing a
45　pencil — first making the leads, then gluing them into grooved cedar-wood slats, shaping the pencils and embossing them with the company name, before packing them into boxes. Although it would have been easier to create the hiding place early in the process, Tee decided that the extra step should be done right at the end to ensure that none of the workforce realised what was going on.

50　After hours and at week-ends, Tee and his fellow managers crept into the factory, took a box of finished pencils off the shelf and carefully drilled out the insides, leaving a short stretch of lead-filled pencil at the working end. Holes drilled, the next job was to slide in the map, fix the metal ferrule to the end, slip in a tiny brass compass and glue the rubber back on top. At the end of the job, the pencil looked just as it had at the start.

55　The maps and compasses arrived secretly at the factory, ready to be inserted into the pencils. The compass was one of Fraser-Smith's early successes. Almost his first job had been to supply a fountain pen with a miniature compass inside. He tackled the problem of the pen first, and once he had established that Platignum could make one with a suitable hiding place, he set about finding a compass to fit it. 'No compass as yet existed that was small enough to fit into
60　the tiny aperture,' he wrote in his autobiography. But in London he discovered 'a couple of back-alley brothers', the Barkers of Clerkenwell, who were making large compasses for the Navy. He asked them to make something 'smaller than they had ever seen or heard of'. They did, and over the next few years the miniature compasses turned up inside pens and pencils, in battledress buttons, hairbrushes and even in place of fillings in airmen's teeth.

65　The next component was the map. Fraser-Smith toyed with handkerchiefs printed with invisible ink that would emerge when soaked with urine. These were too bulky to hide inside gadgets, so he had to think of something else. The maps in the Cumberland pencils were printed on a fine, non-rustling tissue paper made specially for the job, then rolled around a soft wire which was folded over at the tip to secure the paper. Three cotton ties ensured the map
70　stayed tightly rolled and no more than 3 millimetres in diameter. There were four maps — which were fitted into a series of pencils numbered 101 to 104. Pencils labelled 101 held a general map of Germany. The other three concealed larger-scale maps of different sectors of the country.

So did any downed airmen or prisoners find their way home with the help of a Cumberland
75　Pencil? Fraser-Smith was certain his gadgets saved lives and helped people get home, but there were no official records. Officially, he didn't exist. In their remote and tranquil setting in the Lake District, Tee and his colleagues would never find out. Their pencils didn't exist either.

© *New Scientist* — www.newscientist.com

QUESTIONS

Marks Code

1. (i) What is the purpose of the two paragraphs in bold letters which appear before the headline (lines 1–13)? **1 A**

   (ii) How does the sentence structure of lines 1–5 help this purpose? **2 A**

2. How does the writer use word choice in lines 18–20 to suggest secret work? **4 A**

3. Quote the words from lines 25–26 which tell us that Charles Fraser-Smith was not from the Ministry of Supply's Clothing and Textile Department. **1 A**

4. In your own words explain what kind of people might be in need of the pencil maps during World War 2. **3 U**

5. Look at lines 35–37 and also back to lines 10–15.

   Explain in your own words the thinking behind Fraser-Smith's approach to his work. **3 U**

6. What do these words suggest about the atmosphere during World War 2?

   (i) 'bombarded' (line 33),

   (ii) 'conjured' (line 33). **2 A**

7. Why was a pencil a good choice of object for airmen to hide something in? **2 U**

8. Look at lines 47–54.

   How did the need for secrecy make the task of Tee and his fellow managers much more difficult? **1 U**

9. What is suggested about Barkers of Clerkenwell when they are described as 'a couple of back-alley brothers' (lines 60–61)? **2 A**

10. Look at lines 65–70.

    What were the two essential features of the material on which the maps were printed? **2 U**

11. How effective do you find the opening sentence of the last paragraph in keeping your attention to the end of the passage?   **2**   **E**

12. How effective do you find the last sentence as a conclusion to the passage?   **1**   **E**

13. Explain how well the writer has kept us interested in the character of Fraser-Smith throughout the passage?

                                                                                      4   **E**

                                                              Total   **(30)**

NATIONAL
QUALIFICATIONS

Time: 60 minutes

ENGLISH AND
COMMUNICATION
INTERMEDIATE 2
Interpretation

You should attempt all questions.

The total value of the Paper is 30 marks.

The passage that follows was taken from an article in *The Scotsman* newspaper and it discusses a disagreement between the Americans and the people of Dunbar about how the birthplace of a famous environmentalist, John Muir, should be developed.

Read the passage carefully and then answer **all** the questions, **using your own words as far as possible**.

The questions will ask you to show that:

- you understand the main ideas and important details in the passage — in other words, **what** the writer has said (**Understanding — U**).

- you can identify, using appropriate terms, the techniques the writer has used to get across these ideas — in other words, **how** he has said it (**Analysis — A**).

- you can, using appropriate evidence, comment on how effective the writer has been — in other words, **how well** he has said it (**Evaluation — E**).

A code letter (U, A, E) is used alongside each question to make clear its purpose to you. The number of marks attached to each question will give you some idea of the length of answer expected.

DUNBAR FEELS
THE WRATH OF AMERICA

John Muir was an East Lothian lad who became a hero in the US. Now says *Robert Tait*, a plan to gut his birthplace is turning into an international incident.

This risks stating the obvious, but a vast chasm lies between California and Dunbar — geographically, culturally, climatically, and in just about every other way conceivable. It follows therefore that it must take something extra special to get sun-drenched inhabitants of the Golden State exercised about events in a wind-swept small fishing town on the east coast
5   of Scotland.

Step forward John Muir. He has long been a prophet unsung in the land of his birth, obscure to all but the most enthusiastic connoisseurs of Americana. But now a planning row over the proposed redevelopment of the house of his birth in Dunbar has finally brought his messianic status in the US to Scotland's attention.

10   It is controversy rich in irony. Americans, ever the global bullies, trying to impose the insatiable young will of the new world on the unyielding ancient habits of the old. Except that in this case, a mirror image of the stereotypical confrontation is taking place. For it is California, land of the ultra-modern, that is railing against the hidebound Scotland for hatching a hi-tech plan whose spiritual origins lie somewhere between Silicon Valley and Disneyland.

15   The proposal is for a virtual-reality shrine to Muir in the house where he spent the early part of his life, an enterprise which would entail gutting the present structure. Muir's American disciples regard the idea as sacrilege. They cannot believe his Scots compatriots could be so crass and disdainful of the historical actualité

To understand the full dimensions of this disagreement and the passions it arouses in America,
20   it is necessary to get a full picture of a man to whom most Scots have never given a thought.

John Muir, don't you know, is up there in the hallowed pantheon of American greatness. His family left Scotland in 1849, when Muir was 11, and settled in Wisconsin. As a young man, Muir went west, to California where his name was made and his fame endures. His legacy to his adopted homeland is as deeply honoured as anything bestowed by Andrew Carnegie,
25   Alexander Bell or sundry other Scots-Americans.

Muir was America's first great crusading environmentalist and his ability to communicate this creed brought him to Roosevelt's attention, resulting in the two trekking together in Yosemite National Park in 1903. The experience was an inspiration to Roosevelt, a crusading figure himself who shared Muir's passion for the wilderness.

30   Of Muir, Roosevelt later wrote: "He was emphatically a good citizen . . . a man able to influence contemporary thought and action on the subjects to which he had devoted his life. He was a great factor in influencing the thought of California and the thought of the entire country."

    Starting in the 1870s, Muir fashioned modern environmentalism at a time when the concept
35   would have seemed a foreign thought to a generation of Americans preoccupied with exploring the vast untamed yonderland of the new frontier. He foretold man's capacity to wreak awful destruction on the planet. From that knowledge, he inspired the establishment of America's national parks, starting with Yosemite in 1890 and later followed by Mount Rainier, Grand Canyon and Sequoia.

40   Muir was a founder and the first president of the Sierra Club, America's biggest environmental group. With its 600,000 members, most of them well off and highly educated, the Sierra Club carries much influence within the United States — and, the townspeople of Dunbar may be in the process of finding out, possibly beyond it.

    The Sierra Club is now bringing its prodigious organisational capacity to bear on the John Muir
45   Birthplace Trust — set up two years ago to redevelop the house — and the planning department of East Lothian District Council. Alerted by Graham White, a keeper of Muir's memory in Dunbar, some of the the Sierra Club's most enthusiastic and influential activists have swamped the council with impassioned letters decrying a plan which would entail the demolition of a section of the house where Muir's family lived and which is today maintained as it would have
50   looked in the 1840s.

    Elizabeth Pomeroy, a former head of the Sierra Club's Southern California chapter, with 55,000 members, is co-ordinating the letter and e-mail campaign. "What they are planning would be so extreme,' says Pomeroy, who is writing a book about Muir. 'Many Sierra Club members, including myself, have been to the house, but it would be painful for Americans to go there in
55   the future if this is done. They are proposing turning it into a hi-tech exhibit very similar to just logging on to a website."

    "For someone like John Muir, who loved simple and wild places, a hi-tech approach is inappropriate to his legacy. It would be the antithesis of everything he stood for."

    Indeed a quick survey of Muir's life and his assorted writing does prompt the conclusion that
60   the birthplace trustees may have misjudged the character of the man they are trying to honour. This was the man who traversed the globe in the cause of preserving nature's wild creations. As late as 1911 when he was 73, Muir was touring South America and Africa.

    His views on development, whose most corrosive effects he did not live to see, were neatly summed up in his comments on trees. "Any fool can destroy trees," he wrote. "They cannot
65   run away; and if they could, they would still be destroyed — chased and hunted down as long as fun or a dollar could be got out of their bark hides, branching horns, or magnificent bole backbones."

Bill Hanna, Muir's grandson, tells a story, courtesy of his father's childhood memory, that could be a metaphor for how Muir would view the new-fangled plans for his birthplace. In the
70 final years of his life, living in his house in Martinez — in the San Francisco Bay area — that is now preserved as a revered shrine, Muir's meals were prepared by a maid.

Muir complained endlessly about the maid's attempts to boil an egg; it was either too hard or too soft. Eventually, the Muir family bought the maid an egg boiling device that operated by way of a fashionable new invention of the time — electricity. When Muir tasted the product of
75 this new mod con, he hated it. The maid went back to her old way of cooking and Muir never moaned again.

How could such a man have tolerated the thought of his childhood home is falling prey to the forces of economic development?

© *The Scotsman*, 7 July, 2001

QUESTIONS

Marks Code

1. Look carefully at the first paragraph (lines 1–5). How does the writer develop the metaphor of the 'chasm' dividing California from Dunbar?

    2   A

2. Look at lines 10–14.

    Explain why the situation is described as being 'rich in irony'.

    4   U

3. (i)   Explain what the plan is for John Muir's birthplace which has so angered the Americans.

    2   U

    (ii) Why do they think it is wrong?

    1   U

4. Look at lines 6–14.

    Quote two words used about John Muir which suggest that the Americans think of him with almost religious reverence.

    2   A

5. What is the purpose of Paragraph 5 (lines 19–20)?

    1   A

6. Look at lines 34–43.

    (i)   What was the warning given by Muir to the Americans?

    1   U

    (ii) What **TWO** practical steps did he help set in motion to ensure that his aims and ideas would be carried out in the future?

    2   U

7. Which word used in lines 55–56 suggest that Elizabeth Pomeroy does not think of the internet with much respect?

    1   A

8. Look at John Muir's words about cutting down trees in lines 64–67. How do the imagery and word choice make his feelings clear?

    4   A

9. Explain whether you think that the story about his egg being boiled (lines 72–76) makes a good contribution to the argument of the passage.

    2   E

10. How effective do you find the sentence structure of the last paragraph in concluding the passage?　　　　　　　　　　　　　　　　　　　　　　**2**　**E**

11. Whose side do you think the writer is on in the argument? Support your opinion by referring closely to the text.

You should discuss such aspects of the text as: word choice, imagery, sentence structure and tone.　　　　　　　　　　　　　　　　　　　　　　　　**6**　**E**

Total　　**(30)**

NATIONAL
QUALIFICATIONS   Time: 60 minutes

ENGLISH AND
COMMUNICATION
INTERMEDIATE 2
Interpretation

You should attempt all questions.

The total value of the Paper is 30 marks.

The passage that follows was taken from the book *Walking with Dinosaurs* by Tim Haines which was published by BBC Wildlife Ltd. to accompany the television series. It describes the behaviour of one family of dinosaurs, the Diplodocus, which is of the sauropod group.

Read the passage carefully and then answer **all** the questions, **using your own words as far as possible**.

The questions will ask you to show that:

-   you understand the main ideas and important details in the passage — in other words, **what** the writer has said (**Understanding — U**).

-   you can identify, using appropriate terms, the techniques the writer has used to get across these ideas — in other words, **how** he has said it (**Analysis — A**).

-   you can, using appropriate evidence, comment on how effective the writer has been — in other words, **how well** he has said it (**Evaluation — E**).

A code letter (U, A, E) is used alongside each question to make clear its purpose to you. The number of marks attached to each question will give you some idea of the length of answer expected.

Absent Parents

This upland Laurasian forest is the nursery for the giant sauropod herds of the plains. When they are very small the sauropodlets exploit the lowest ground level vegetation in the forest. Here there is plenty of food ranging from liverworts, club mosses, moss and fungus to a number of delicate species of small ferns. There are also larger ferns, such as the king fern, that have highly nutritious stems. The sauropodlet will have to learn fast what is and isn't good to eat if she is to pile on the weight as fast as she needs to. As she progresses further into the forest and the yolk in her stomach is used up, she begins to pick at the plants around her, so starting a lifetime obsession with feeding.

Out on the plains, the sauropodlet's mother is already almost 100 kilometres away from her hatchling's struggle for survival. She is part of a herd of adult Diplodocus grazing on cycads in the hot Jurassic sun. Of all the sauropods, Diplodocus are perhaps the most elegant. Even the oldest animals weigh only about 25 tonnes, half as much as the bulkier species such as Brachiosaurus. Yet they can grow to be twice as long as Brachiosaurus, about 40-45 metres. This is partly due to an extraordinarily long, flexible tail, which for the last 3 or 4 metres is no more than a long thin whip.

Diplodocus are also unique in that they produce a very distinctive range of sounds to help them communicate with each other while they continue feeding, with their heads buried deep in ferns. The strangest of these sounds is felt rather than heard by the rest of the herd — a very low-frequency rumble that travels through the ground and is sensed by other Diplodocus through their feet. It is believed that this is a way of keeping the herd together. As long as each member can feel the others rumbling nearby, even if he can't see them, he feels reassured. The pitch is too low for most creatures to pick up, but close to the herd the rumbles are strong enough to make sand dance on stone and plants vibrate

The deepest and strongest rumbles come from the females, who dominate Diplodocus herds. They are larger than the males and, because size matters in a world full of powerful predators, they tend to live longer. This particular herd contains one gigantic old female. She is by far the longest creature there and must be at least 100 years old. Many of the spines that run down her back are broken and twisted, and her flanks are criss-crossed with scars from decades of predator attacks, but her sheer size now makes her almost invincible. Except for the odd wandering male, all Diplodocus live in herds, bound together by the need for mutual protection. Large, old females are an extraordinary asset, providing security for many other smaller Diplodocus. There are just under 40 sauropods in this herd and most are subadults ranging from six to 15 years old; there are no really young animals. When the herd is on the move, the smaller animals tend to follow the larger females, sometimes walking right under their long tails, for protection.

The old female has led the herd to the cycad grove, where they are now feeding. Besides the low rumbles, there are lots of other sounds being produced — a range of audible snorts that get deeper and deeper the larger the animal is, and the constant eerie swish and crack of their tails.

40 Diplodocus use their whip-like tails as highly sophisticated communication devices. As with the rumbling, the tail carries on a conversation while the head is buried in vegetation 30 metres away. With a gentle flick of the base the thin end of the tail can be accelerated so fast that it whistles through the air and produces a supersonic whip-crack. If several members of a herd perform the same trick, the noise can be considerable, and this is a first line of defence when they are threatened by predators. Although they avoid making direct contact with

45 attackers, the aggressive cracking is often enough to see off all but the most determined. The tails also maintain a tactile communication within the herd, constantly exploring the backs of other members. In fact, it often appears that the more tails an individual can feel, the calmer he is. If a Diplodocus begins to feel isolated, he will swish his tail or snort to attract attention before he bothers to lift his head from feeding.

50 As a background to all this snorting, rumbling, swishing and cracking is another noise — the deep gurgle and grind of very active stomachs. The Diplodocus' gut is one of the secrets of its success. Indeed, all sauropods benefit from having this huge food processor, which allows them to feed and extract nutrients from some of the most unpalatable food imaginable. The stomach of a Diplodocus can hold over half a tonne of vegetation. In addition, it contains several

55 kilograms of stones, which are used to keep the food turning over and grind it down further. All this digestive activity is clearly audible outside the animal and adds a particular character to the sound of a Diplodocus herd.

The herd has been attracted to the cycad grove by the flush of new leaves. Cycads are most unattractive plants to the majority of grazing animals. Their bark is as tough as armour, their

60 leaves are thick and spiny, and they produce a range of poisons to make themselves even more unpalatable. However, their new leaves are soft and more easily grazed. These grow from a central crown on top of the plant and are protected by a ring of older leaves around the outside. But the Diplodocus reach over these with their long necks and pluck at the crown within. Securing each long leaf stem with their peglike teeth, they strip upwards, removing and

65 swallowing all the soft new growth. The older spiny leaves have little effect because the Diplodocus' soft nostrils are placed well out of the way on top of their heads. Cycads have evolved to overcome this threat by growing their flush of new leaves very quickly, so that they are less likely to be discovered by a grazing animal during their vulnerable period. Unfortunately this grove of cycads has been unsuccessful and the Diplodocus are feasting.

© Tim Haines, 1999

QUESTIONS

Marks Code

1. Look at the first paragraph (lines 1–8).

    (i)   What is the aim of the young sauropod from the time it is born and how does it set about achieving that aim? **2 U**

    (ii) What does the word 'obsession' suggest about the sauropods' attitude to food? **1 A**

    (iii) Quote a phrase (10 words) from earlier in the paragraph which explains this attitude. **1 A**

2. Look at the first sentence of paragraph 2.

    How has the writer managed to arouse our sympathies for the young sauropod? **2 A**

3. 'Elegant' (line 11).

    Which aspect of the Diplodocus make this expression seem surprising? **1 A**

4. Look at paragraph 3 (lines 16–23).

    How do members of the herd keep in contact when they cannot see each other? **2 U**

5. Explain **TWO** reasons for the importance of the old female in the herd? **2 U**

6. How do the words round about 'predators' (line 25) help to make its meaning clear? **2 U**

7. Look at paragraph 6 (lines 39–49).

    (i) What appear to be the **TWO** main uses for the Diplodocus' tails? **2 U**

    (ii) Explain how the writer uses imagery and sound effects to help us to imagine what the tails of the dinosaurs were like. **4 A**

8. 'huge food processor' (line 52)

    To what extent do you find this an effective image to describe the Diplodocus' stomachs? **2 E**

9. Look at lines 58–68.

    (i)   What protections have the cycad trees developed over the centuries?   **2**   U

    (ii)   Why can the Diplodocus easily overcome these protections?   **1**   U

10. 'The Diplodocus are feasting.' Do you think that this makes a good ending for the extract?   **2**   E

11. How well has the writer managed to make us imagine animals that neither he nor we have ever seen in the flesh?

You might wish to refer to word choice, imagery, sentence structure, anecdote, sound effects, etc.   **4**   E

Total   **(30)**

Marks Code

1. **Why might what is spoken of in paragraph 1 be described as ironical?**   2   U

We would expect a man who had made such a marvellous invention would be praised and
respected.
Instead he is thrown into prison.

One mark for each side of the irony.

2. **Look at lines 5–7. How does the word choice help us to realise how difficult the first bicycle**
    was to control?   2   A
    'ungainly' suggests something awkward and unbalanced.
    'inadvertently' suggests that he did not intend to steer in this direction, the bicycle had a will of its
    own.

    One mark each for the explanation. 0 marks for just picking out the words.

3. **Look carefully at paragraph 4 (lines 11–14).**

    (i) **In your own words, explain what Macmillan had hoped to gain from his journey to**
         Gorbals, Glasgow?   1   U
         He hoped to get someone with money and enterprise to develop his bicycle commercially.

    (ii) **In your own words explain the effect it had on his family.**   3   U
         'notoriety' — it made them well known but in the bad sense.
         'ridicule' — the family was held up to mockery.
         'shame and embarrassment' — they felt humiliated.

         One mark for each separate point. No marks for quotation.

4. **Explain the significance of the magistrate's actions after the court case (lines 19–21)** 2   U
    The magistrate was clearly a well educated and important person.
    It showed that though he felt obliged to fulfil his duties as a magistrate he recognised the brilliance
    of the invention.

    One mark for the idea of recognising the brilliance.
    One mark for either the idea of his cleverness OR one mark for the idea that he felt obliged to
    follow through the legal system.

5. **Look carefully at paragraph 11 (lines 33–35). How does the sentence structure help to**
    emphasise the point the writer is trying to make about the bicycle?   2   A
    The first part of the sentence is complicated and awkward, with phrases separated by commas, just
    like the appearance of the bicycle.
    The ending is clear and short. It states the only thing that mattered; the bicycle worked.
    There is a dramatic pause caused by the dash which leads to the important point at the end.

    Two separate comments for the full marks.

Marks Code

6. **Look at lines 42–48 :**

   Explain why you think that the 'hobby horse' was given that name?   2   A

   Alliteration makes it sound cheerful and pleasant.

   It was only for sport so it was given the name for an unimportant activity.

   'hobby' sound a bit like 'hoppy'. It was a cross between a horse and a person, etc.

   Any reasonable suggestion for one mark; with supporting explanation for another mark.

7. **Which word in paragraph 16 (lines 49–52) sums up the general opinion of the 'hobby horse'**
   made by Macmillan and his friend?   1   A

   'bizarre'.

8. **How does the word choice and imagery of paragraph 19 (lines 58–61) make clear to us**
   people's reaction to the machine?   4   A

   'devilish machine' — they thought it was supernatural and evil, as though from Hell.

   'fear and horror' — it seemed so awful to them that it was something that actually made them
   afraid and disgusted.

   'The laddie's daft' — suggests a more down to earth reaction, blaming the boy for making
   something so absurd.

   'changed their tune' — a more cheerful expression to show that they switched sides when they saw
   its success.

   One mark each if 4 points made briefly. Two marks for a well made point.

9. **Look at lines 65–67.**

   How does the writer make clear his attitude towards Gavin Dalzell and Thomas McCall?   2   A

   'shamelessly' suggests he thinks they should be ashamed of themselves and he despises them for
   their theft of the idea.

   The idea of a 'tidy sum' might be developed instead and a discussion of their commercialism based
   on the £7 and £1,000 but the <u>writer's attitude</u> must be discussed.

   One mark for his attitude and one mark for an explanation of the evidence.

10. **From your reading of the passage as a whole and in your own words explain any TWO**
    benefits that were to be gained from the bicycle.   2   U

    It could be worked by a man's own power.

    It could go comparatively long distances.

    It could go faster than a coach.

11. **How well does the writer make clear his liking for the character of Kirkpatrick Macmillan**
    in this article?   3   E

    The writer tells stories that reflect on an easy going character: he does not mind the fine; he does
    not bother to sell the patent of the bicycle, etc.

    The writer shows his determination as he keeps working in spite of being laughed at.

    The writer demonstrates Macmillan's generosity to friends and even a duke.

    The writer shows that he was popular by his comment on the funeral.

    Three points briefly developed for one mark each. One point very fully developed could get the
    three marks.

12. **How well in your opinion has the writer Jeremy Hodges demonstrated his skill in presenting the early history of the bicycle?**
Justify your answer by referring to, for example, use of detail, word choice and imagery, sentence structure, anecdote, etc.   **4**   **E**

The writer concentrates on the character of the inventor which makes it more personal.

He gives dates, facts but among quite a chatty account.

He describes the bicycle in some detail, using accurate word choice to make it clear to us.

He makes clear the reaction of others.

He tells anecdotes to make the story more interesting.

                                                          Total   **(30)**

ANSWERS TO PASSAGE B

Marks Code

1. **Explain the tone of the opening sentence ('My subject this week').**   2   A
    Sarcastic or ironic — the contrast between the high tone of 'contribution to' and 'development of'
    with the subject of bin bags.
    Humorous an acceptable answer.

    One mark for tone; one mark for explanation.

2. **What is the 'paradox' described in the second paragraph?**   2   U
    The contradiction is that we cannot do without bin bags, but they are designed to be thrown away.

    Both sides of the contradiction must be stated for the marks.

3. **'inextricably subsumed' (line 5)**
    'orgy of disposal' (line 7)
    How does each of these phrases help to create the atmosphere of moving house?   4   A
    Both phrases suggest the confusion and loss which occurs when moving house but also the
    pleasure of making a new start.
    'inextricably subsumed' suggests that things have disappeared from sight under other things and
    are so tangled up that they may never appear again.
    'orgy of disposal' suggests intense almost wild enjoyment caused by throwing things out.

    One mark for general comment. Two marks each for the full explanations.

4. **What is the function of paragraph 4 (line 12)?**   2   A
    'But' indicates a change from the general introductory discussion about bin bags.
    He is introducing the main point of his article, i.e., the connection between bin bags and the car
    industry.

    One mark for indication of change (turning point) and one mark for the idea of introducing the
    main topic.

5. **Look at the character of Sarah as depicted between lines 13–17. In what way is she typical**   2   U
    of a modern woman and in what way not?
    Typical in that she is interested in cars and helps her boyfriend with his.
    Not typical in that she does not own or drive a car herself.

    Other reasons might be suggested, in fact, even the idea that she is environmentally aware and is
    therefore typical of a modern woman might be suggested. If the suggestion is supported by
    argument it should be accepted.

    Contrast should be suggested for full marks.

6. **Look at the sentence structure in lines 19–21 ('And . . . door')**
    How effective do you find the way the writer has written these sentences?   2   E
    Comments should be made on one of these: the dramatic pause caused by the repeated full stops;
    on the interruption to the words of Sara and on the use of 'And' to start his own statement.

    An assessment of the effect of one of these for the two marks.

7. **Explain what the expression "God rest its bones' (line 23) tells us is the author's attitude to his first car?** 2 A

Respect is suggested by the reference to God.

He thinks of it as human and is affectionate is suggested by the reference to its bones.

Nostalgia is suggested by his emotional memory of it.

One mark each or an attitude which is justified.

8. **Explain the writer's reference to his innocence in lines 25–26?** 2 U

We always assume that there is a reason for something, that the car manufacturers, for example, know best.

Clearly there is no reason for the bin bag to be there but he accepts the idea, like a child believing everything an adult says, that it should be there and replaces it with another one.

9. **Look at lines 40–45**

What does the writer suggest is the real reason for the bin bags being used inside car doors? 2 U

He suggests that because there is no longer so much paper used in offices, the car companies have a surplus of bin bags and because they cannot be disposed of in an environmentally friendly way they are hiding them all in car doors to save their image.

One mark for the idea of surplus bin bags. One mark for firms trying to appear environmentally friendly. Credit should be given for the idea of image being important to car manufacturers.

10. **Look at lines 48-53.**

(i) **How does the word choice help to create the writer's attitude to the Bentley car?** 2 A

He feels great admiration and respect for it, 'trembling hand' suggests it makes him nervous.

'Beautifully inlaid' suggests he appreciates its almost antique splendour.

(ii) **How does the writer use word choice to make his point about the bin bag inside the Bentley's door?** 2 A

'Not a bespoke . . . caviar jar disposal bag' tells us what he expected from so up-market a car, caviar being supposedly the food of the rich.

'normal' brings us down to earth and 'congealed cheese sauce' makes it seem sordid like old, disgusting, cheap food.

2 E

11. **How effective do you find the final one word paragraph as a conclusion to this article?**

It is short and to the point.

It sums up the question he has been asking all the way through.

It makes clear that he still does not know the answer.

His readers are being invited to send him an explanation.

Some might say they wanted the answer and think an inconclusive article is pointless.

For the two marks the answer should refer in some way to the rest of the passage.

Marks Code

12. **In this passage the writer is trying to discuss a not very serious issue in an entertaining way. By commenting on at least TWO techniques, explain how well you think he has achieved his purpose.**   **4   E**

He uses stories

He uses personal experience.

Sentence structure is short and mostly simple.

He uses humour.

He refers to things we have all heard of: Bostik, Blue Peter, etc.

Each should be explained for full marks.

Total   (30)

ACKNOWLEDGEMENTS

We hereby acknowledge the use of copyright material in this book
and are grateful to those for granting this permission.

Extract of an article by Jeremy Hodges
which appeared in *The Scotsman.*

Article entitled *Opening the door to a weird use of bin bags*
by James May
which appeared in *Scotland on Sunday.*

Article entitled *If it's good to talk, why all the scares over health?*
by Camillo Fracassini.
Reprinted by permission of The Scotsman Publications Limited.

Article entitled *The height of nonsense*
© Julian Champkin.
Reprinted by permission of Times Newspapers Limited.

Article entitled *Don't feed the bears*
by Tim Cornwell.
Reprinted by permission of The Scotsman Publications Limited.

Article entitled *Relaxation can really get on an athlete's nerves at times*
by Ian Wood, sports columnist with *The Scotsman.*

Article entitled *Has the Age of Ageism had its day?*
by Gavin Esler, writer and broadcaster.
This article was part of his regular weekly column for *The Scotsman.*

Article entitled *Secret service*
by Stephanie Pain.
Reprinted by permission of *New Scientist.*
www.newscientist.com

Article entitled *Dunbar feels the wrath of America*
by Robert Tait.
Reprinted by permission of The Scotsman Publications Limited.

The extract from *Walking with Dinosaurs*
by Tim Haines reprinted on pages 54–55
is reproduced with the permission of BBC Worldwide Limited.
Copyright © Tim Haines 1999.

Printed by Bell & Bain Ltd., Glasgow, Scotland, U.K.